D0904893

SandCastle

Word Families Set 6

-ing as in king

Pam Scheunemann

Consulting Editor Monica Marx, M.A./Reading Specialist

Publishing Company

Published by SandCastle™, an imprint of ABDO Publishing Company, 4940 Viking Drive, Edina, Minnesota 55435.

Printed in the United States.

Credits
Edited by: Pam Price
Curriculum Coordinator: Nancy Tuminelly
Cover and Interior Design and Production: Mighty Media
Photo Credits: Brand X Pictures, Comstock, Corbis Images, Digital Vision, Hemera, PhotoDisc, Rubberball Productions

Library of Congress Cataloging-in-Publication Data

Scheunemann, Pam, 1955-
       -Ing as in king / Pam Scheunemann.
          p. cm. -- (Word families. Set VI)
       Summary: Introduces, in brief text and illustrations, the use of the letter combination "ing" in such words as "king," "ring," "wring," and "swing."
       ISBN 1-59197-256-6
       1. Readers (Primary) [1. Vocabulary. 2. Reading.] I. Title.

PE1119 .S435156 2003
428.1--dc21   4-10-03   2002038223

SandCastle™ books are created by a professional team of educators, reading specialists, and content developers around five essential components that include phonemic awareness, phonics, vocabulary, text comprehension, and fluency. All books are written, reviewed, and leveled for guided reading, early intervention reading, and Accelerated Reader® programs and designed for use in shared, guided, and independent reading and writing activities to support a balanced approach to literacy instruction.

Let Us Know

After reading the book, SandCastle would like you to tell us your stories about reading. What is your favorite page? Was there something hard that you needed help with? Share the ups and downs of learning to read. We want to hear from you! To get posted on the ABDO Publishing Company Web site, send us e-mail at:

sandcastle@abdopub.com

SandCastle Level: Beginning

-ing Words

bring

ring

sing

spring

string

wing

3

Jim taught Rover to
bring the slipper.

Tim gave Sandy a wedding ring.

Mom, Dawn, and Jill
like to sing.

Kelly loves flowers in the spring.

Miki likes to play with the string.

The bird hides its head
under its wing.

The King's Journey

There once
was a very
old king.

12

He lived in a castle
high above everything.

It was so high
he couldn't see a thing.

So he set off
on a journey
one spring.

The king
saw a girl
on a swing.

Then he
saw a boy
with a kite
on a string.

Above him
was a bird
with a bee
on its wing.

Then the king
heard a bell ring.

THIS
WAY TO
KING'S
CASTLE

It was time to head
home from his fling.

Along his way, he
heard people sing.

The queen was happy to see the king!

He said, "Now I've seen everything!"

The -ing Word Family

anything	something
bring	spring
cling	sting
everything	string
fling	swing
king	thing
ring	wing
sing	wring

Glossary

Some of the words in this list may have more than one meaning. The meaning listed here reflects the way the word is used in the book.

bring   to take or carry something to another place

fling   a brief period of enjoyment

journey   a trip or vacation

string   a cord made of fiber used to tie things together

swing   a seat that hangs by rope that you can sit on and move back and forth

About SandCastle™

A professional team of educators, reading specialists, and content developers created the SandCastle™ series to support young readers as they develop reading skills and strategies and increase their general knowledge. The SandCastle™ series has four levels that correspond to early literacy development in young children. The levels are provided to help teachers and parents select the appropriate books for young readers.

Emerging Readers
(no flags)

Beginning Readers
(1 flag)

Transitional Readers
(2 flags)

Fluent Readers
(3 flags)

These levels are meant only as a guide. All levels are subject to change.

To see a complete list of SandCastle™ books and other nonfiction titles from ABDO Publishing Company, visit **www.abdopub.com** or contact us at:

4940 Viking Drive, Edina, Minnesota 55435 • 1-800-800-1312 • fax: 1-952-831-1632